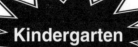

# From Your Friends At The MAILBOX®

# MARCH

## A MONTH OF REPRODUCIBLES AT

### Kindergarten

**Editor:**
Angie Kutzer

**Writers:**
Susan Bunyan, Lucia Kemp Henry, Angie Kutzer

**Art Coordinator:**
Clevell Harris

**Artists:**
Cathy Spangler Bruce, Teresa Davidson,
Nick Greenwood, Clevell Harris, Sheila Krill,
Rob Mayworth, Kimberly Richard,
Barry Slate, Donna K. Teal

**Cover Artist:**
Jennifer Tipton Bennett

www.themailbox.com

©1998 by THE EDUCATION CENTER, INC.
All rights reserved.
ISBN #1-56234-227-4

Manufactured in the United States
10 9 8 7 6 5 4 3

# Table Of Contents

Meetings:

To Do:

Special Dates:

Books To Check Out:

MARCH
Classroom Themes:

Materials To Collect:

Birthdays:

Duties This Month:

# MARCH

©1998 The Education Center, Inc. • *March Monthly Reproducibles* • Kindergarten • TEC943

# In Like A Lion, Out Like A Lamb!

March's unpredictable weather can roar one day and "baa" the next. This lion and lamb proverb provides the perfect opportunity to practice opposites with your little ones.

## Have You Any Wool?

Yes sir, yes sir, wool that's full of opposites! Duplicate page 6 for each child. Have her cut out the wool pieces and glue each one to its correct sheep, matching the opposite picture to the one on each of the lions. What a "woolly" good job!

## Opposites Attract

Opposites end up being a perfect match in this self-checking activity. Duplicate pages 7 and 8 onto white construction paper for each child. Direct him to color the pictures on the wheel holder, then cut out all of the pieces. Help the child glue a shape wheel back-to-back to each opposite-picture wheel so that the triangle on shape wheel 1 is directly behind the happy face on picture wheel 1 and the triangle on shape wheel 2 is directly behind the sad face on picture wheel 2. Fold the wheel holder in half; then cut out the windows through both thicknesses of the paper. Attach the wheels to the holder where indicated with brads. Encourage the child to use the wild and woolly wheels to test his knowledge of opposites.

## Score With A Roar!

Youngsters will never go "baa-ck" to playing tic-tac-toe the old way after you introduce this textured version. Simply cut squares of craft fur for the lion team and provide cotton balls for the lamb team. Here we go, for three in a row!

# Have You Any Wool?

Cut.

Match the opposites.

Glue.

Color.

©1998 The Education Center, Inc. • *March Monthly Reproducibles* • Kindergarten • TEC943

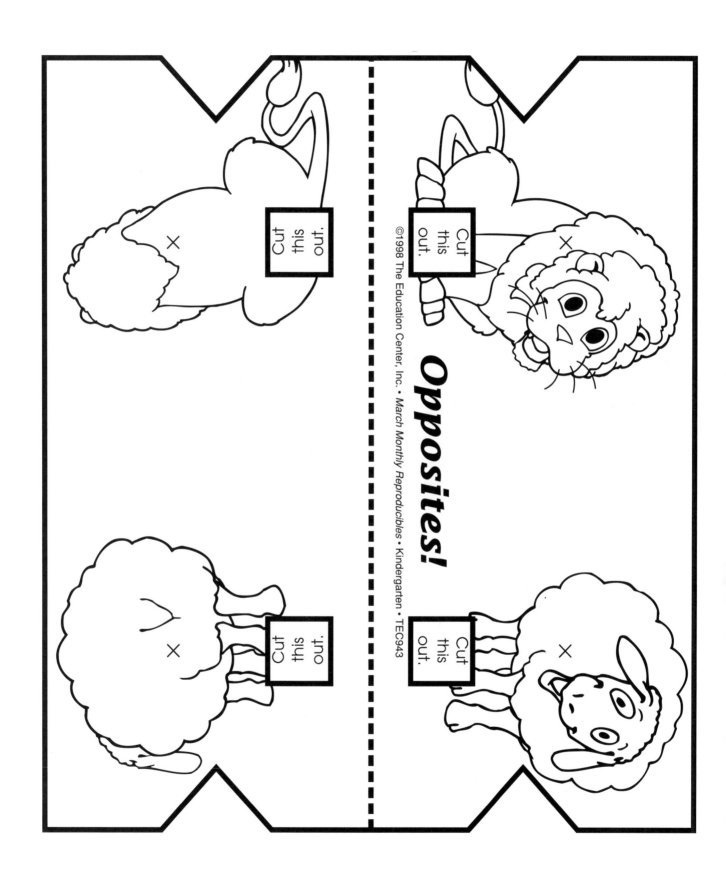

Cut this out.

Cut this out.

Cut this out.

Cut this out.

©1998 The Education Center, Inc. • March Monthly Reproducibles • Kindergarten • TEC943

Opposites!

# Shape Wheels
Use with "Opposites Attract" on page 5.

# Opposite-Picture Wheels
Use with "Opposites Attract" on page 5.

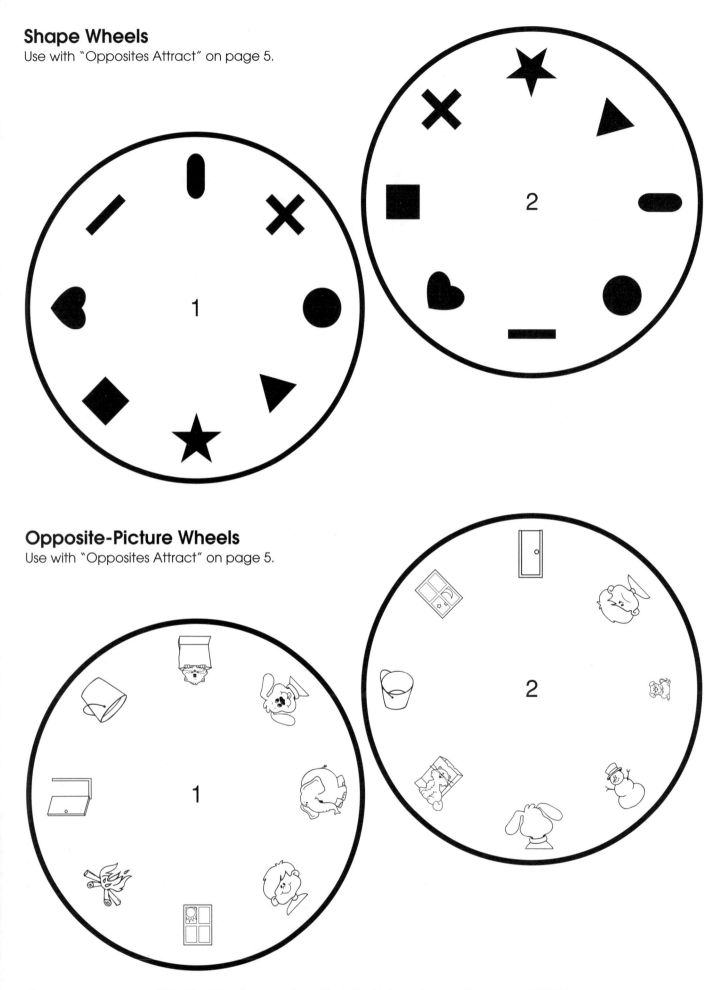

# NATIONAL NUTRITION MONTH®

National Nutrition Month® (March 1–31) is a great time to focus on helping your youngsters learn to make healthful food choices. Add a little spice to your favorite nutrition lessons by mixing in the following activities.

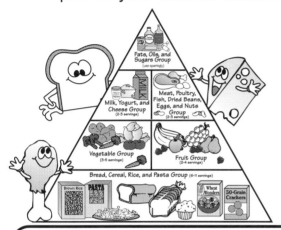

## Pyramid Kids

Use the United States Department of Agriculture's Food Guide Pyramid to give youngsters a simple, visual outline of what to eat each day. After discussing the pyramid with your students, lay an enlarged copy or a poster of the pyramid on the floor. Invite each child to take a turn tossing a beanbag onto the pyramid. Have her name the food group on which the beanbag lands and an item that belongs in that food group. Soon every kid will know the pyramid!

## Good Food Booklet

Your youngsters will acquire an appetite for good food choices when they put together these nutrition reference booklets. Duplicate pages 10–16 onto white construction paper for each child. (You can have your students construct the whole booklet on the same day as a culminating activity; or complete each page as you discuss that particular food group during the unit, then compile the pages at the end of the unit.) Have each child cut out the booklet pages and pieces, glue each piece to the appropriate page where indicated, and then color the pictures. Read the text aloud and direct the child to complete each page by drawing his favorite food from that designated group. Complete the cover as described below; then stack the pages in order and staple them together at the left. For illustrations with more variety, gather the materials needed for the ideas below and help each child complete each page as described.

**Cover:** Cut a brown lunch bag in half as shown, and then trim one of the halves to three inches in height. Personalize the paper-bag piece; then glue it to the cover so that the bottom edge of the bag touches the bottom edge of the cover. Color, cut out, and glue the bread and apple pictures to the cover above the bag. Fill the bag by drawing more healthful foods around the bread and apple.

**Page 1:** Glue on an assortment of real pasta pieces.

**Page 2:** Draw a favorite fruit using scented markers.

**Page 3:** Dip a cut vegetable in paint and make a veggie print.

**Page 4:** Cut the front panel from a clean, empty milk carton and glue it to the page.

**Page 5:** Look through grocery store advertisements to find a picture of a favorite protein food. Cut the picture out and glue it to the page.

**Page 6:** Draw and color a favorite healthful snack on the page.

# My Good Food Book

Staple pages together here.

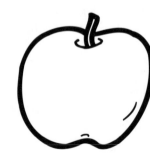

 Cut.

 Glue.

1

Eat lots of bread, cereal, rice, and pasta.

 Cut.  Glue.

2

Fruit is sweet to eat and healthful, too!

Cut.

Glue.

3

Vegetables
are
yummy and
good
for you!

 Cut.  Glue.

4

Eat dairy foods for calcium.

MILK

Yogurt

Cut.    Glue.

5

Try meats, beans eggs, nuts, poultry... yum!

  Cut.    Glue.

6

What
healthful
snacks
do you
like?

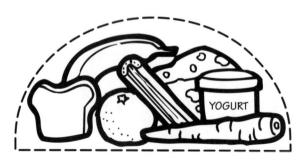

YOGURT

 Cut.

 Glue.

# NATIONAL PIG DAY

Oink! Oink! Celebrate one of man's most intelligent and useful domesticated animals on March 1—pigs! Use your favorite version of *The Three Little Pigs* and the following activities to root up some fun in your classroom.

## Who's Afraid Of The Big, Bad Wolf?

Not *your* youngsters when they see him just hanging around the classroom. Enlist the help of several students to construct one of these storytelling mobiles. (You may want to make several mobiles, each one with a different group of children so that everyone has a chance to contribute.)

**Materials Needed For Each Mobile:**
— one 10" x 3" strip of craft foam, cardboard, or tagboard
— construction-paper copies of the patterns on pages 18 and 19 (You will need to duplicate the house pattern three times.)
— 4 pieces of yarn (two 16" lengths, one 20" length, and one 8" length)
— straw or raffia

— sticks or brown pipe-cleaner pieces
— small, red rectangles (bricks) cut from craft foam or construction paper
— 1 brad fastener
— scissors
— crayons
— glue
— hole puncher

**Directions:**
1. Color the wolf and pig faces.
2. Cut out all of the construction-paper pieces.
3. Glue a different material—straw, sticks, or bricks—onto each house.
4. Punch holes where indicated on each of the patterns.
5. Punch four holes in the foam strip as shown.
6. Attach the wolf to the top of the strip with a brad.
7. Tie the ends of the shortest yarn length together; then loop it through the top of the wolf for hanging.
8. Tie one end of the longest yarn length to the hole in the middle of the strip.
9. Tie one end of each of the remaining yarn lengths to the other two holes on the strip.
10. Thread each pig through a different piece of yarn.
11. Tie each house to the end of a different piece of yarn.

Hang the mobiles just out of students' reach. Then watch them huff and puff as they blow the mobiles around!

## A New Spin On An Old Story

After reading *The Three Little Pigs,* play this educational version of Spin The Bottle. To prepare, duplicate the questions on page 20 onto construction paper and cut them apart. Insert the questions into a small, clean plastic soda or water bottle. Set the bottle in the middle of a circle of seated children.

Start the game by spinning the bottle. When the bottle stops, have the child to whom the lid end of the bottle is pointing open the bottle and remove a question. Read the question to the child. After she answers it, invite her to spin the bottle for the next round of play.

17

# Patterns
Use with "Who's Afraid Of The Big, Bad Wolf?" on page 17.

# Question Strips

Use with "A New Spin On An Old Story" on page 17.

| | |
|---|---|
| Where did the pigs live at the beginning of the story? | Was the story "real" or "make-believe"? |
| "Not by the hair of" what? | Which house could not be blown down? |
| Which pig was the smartest? | What happened to the wolf at the end of the story? |
| What did the pigs want to build? | How did the pig get away from the wolf at the fair? |
| What did the third pig use to build his house? | The wolf invited the pig to pick turnips and what else? |
| What did the second pig use to build his house? | How many characters were there in the story? |
| What did the first pig use to build his house? | How many houses were built in the story? |
| Which two houses did the wolf blow down? | What is your own house made of? |
| What did the wolf say when he blew on the houses? | Where do you think the wolf lived? |
| What was the wolf going to do with the pigs? | What sound does a pig make? |

**Note To The Teacher:** Read through the questions before inserting them in the bottle to make sure each one can be answered with your version of *The Three Little Pigs.*

# HAPPY BIRTHDAY, DR. SEUSS!

Oh, the places you can go with Dr. Seuss books! Celebrate the man behind that coercive cat in the striped hat on March 2—Dr. Seuss's birthday. Use the following activities to make it a "wubbulous" day!

## NOW *THAT* IS A HAT

Use the patterns on page 22 to create a hat full of Dr. Seuss. Duplicate the patterns several times on red and white construction paper; then cut them out. Glue a hat brim to the bottom of a large sheet of paper. Each time you read a Dr. Seuss book to your youngsters, write its title on a stripe. Glue the stripes to the hat, forming a red/white pattern. Try to make the hat as tall as possible in one day (preferably March 2—Dr. Seuss's birthday), or continue for a week, a month, or the whole year!

## WWW.WUBBULOUS

Take students on an Internet field trip to Seussville for some nifty learning games and activities. You will also find some teaching ideas, contest descriptions, an events calendar, and an on-line catalog! The address is *www.seussville.com*. Be sure to check out the site before using it with your students. Because of the constant changes and updates, you never know when the site may be replaced.

## JUST IMAGINE!

Many of Dr. Seuss's lovable, zany characters have something in common—they come from his imagination. Encourage your youngsters' imaginations with these new creations. Give them several fictitious names, such as Bubbalump, Giffandorf, and Sumpadunk. Have each child choose a name and draw what she thinks it looks like. Then have her share her drawing with the class and tell more about her creation—where it lives, what it does, what it eats, etc.

A Sumpadunk eats grass and can fly.

# Hat Patterns
Use with "Now *That* Is A Hat" on page 21.

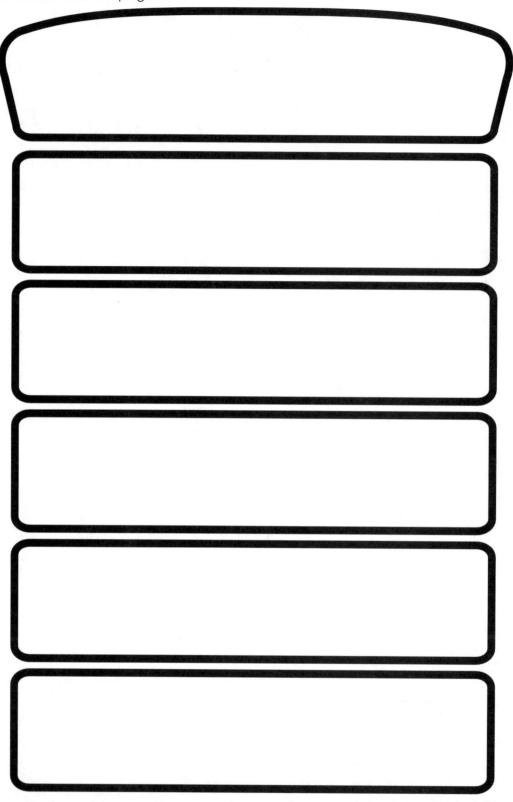

DR. SEUSS—ON THE LOOSE!

# NEWSPAPER IN EDUCATION WEEK

Extra, extra! Here are some front-page activities using newspapers. Consider trying them out during Newspaper In Education Week, observed annually during the first full week in March.

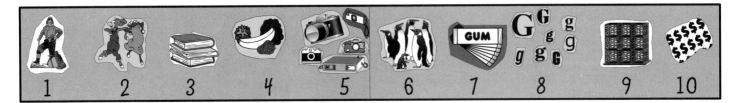

| 1 | 2 | 3 | 4 | 5 | 6 | 7 | 8 | 9 | 10 |

## Numbers In The News

Here's an idea that reinforces set recognition, counting, and sequencing. For each child, cut a sheet of 12" x 18" construction paper in half lengthwise; then tape the ends together to make a 6" x 36" strip. Have the child look through the newspaper and cut out ten sets of objects, each set showing a different number from one to ten. Direct the child to glue the sets in numerical order to his strip, then label each set with the corresponding numeral. Now that's news you can count on!

## Who Can Find...?

The race is on to be the first child to find the sight word you ask for in this activity. Label each of a supply of flash cards with a different sight word. Give each child a section of newspaper. Hold up a card and say, "Who can find the word [_can_]?" Direct each child to look through her paper, put her finger on the designated word when she finds it, and raise her hand. Invite the winner to choose the next word for the class to find.

## Newspaper Search

Send your youngsters on a scavenger hunt through the newspaper. Duplicate page 24 for each child. Provide access to a supply of newspapers. Read aloud the list of items that the children are to find. Direct each child to cut out the designated items and glue them to the appropriate spaces on his page. As a bonus, have each child find the letters in his first name, cut them out, and glue them in order on the back of his page.

23

Name _____

## The Search Is On!

Look through the newspaper.
Can you find…

DAILY NEWS
Context Clues Tell All!

| | |
|---|---|
| the numeral 9? | a ball? |
| a car? | a sight word? | the weather? |
| a child? | a shape? | an animal? |

**Bonus Box:** Find and cut out the letters in your first name and glue them in order on the back of your paper.

# St. Patrick's Day

What's Irish, festive, and green all over? St. Patrick's Day, of course! Celebrate the observance on March 17 with these ideas for your lucky little learners.

## Lots O' Green!

Other youngsters will be green with envy when they see these booklets your students make. Gather the following materials together: a class supply of paint stirrers, green paint (optional), green glitter, Elmer's® GluColors™ in green, green tissue paper, two brads per child, St. Patrick's Day stickers, crayons, glue, scissors, and access to a stapler. For each child, duplicate the booklet cover on page 26 twice (once with the words masked out) onto green construction paper. Then duplicate pages 27–30 onto white construction paper.

To construct a booklet, paint or color a paint stirrer green. Cut out all of the booklet pages and the leprechaun pieces. Glue the back cover of the booklet to the top of the paint stirrer. Write your name where indicated on the front cover of the booklet; then decorate it with green glitter. Use the colored glue to fill in the shamrocks on page 1. Color the tree on page 2; then glue small balls of tissue paper to the tree. Color the leprechaun on page 3; then attach each of his arms to the page with a brad. Draw yourself wearing green on page 4; then color the picture and embellish with St. Patrick's Day stickers. After the glue dries, sequence the pages between the two covers and staple them together at the top.

## A Lucky Limerick

Encourage your future poets to create one of these humorous verses named after the city of Limerick, Ireland. Duplicate page 31 for each child. Write her dictation as she fills in the blanks. Then invite her to illustrate her poem and share it with the class. Display the rollicking rhymes on a St. Patrick's Day bulletin board.

## St. Patrick's Patterns

Spread a little green across the curriculum with this math activity. Duplicate page 32 for each child. Have her cut the St. Patrick's Day symbols apart where indicated. Then direct her to complete each pattern by gluing the appropriate symbol in the corresponding box. As an extension, encourage the child to go for the gold and use the leftover pieces to create a pattern of her own on the back of her paper. Reward efforts with chocolates wrapped in gold foil.

LOTS LOTS O' GREEN! by _____

©1998 The Education Center, Inc. • March Monthly Reproducibles • Kindergarten • TEC943

Green on the shamrocks.

1

Green on the tree.

2

Green on the leprechaun.

3

Use with "Lots O' Green!" on page 25.

Green on me!

4

©1998 The Education Center, Inc. • *March Monthly Reproducibles* • Kindergarten • TEC943

Name _____

# A Lucky Limerick

There once was a _____ we've been told,

Who wore a green _____ in the cold.

While wandering around,

A leprechaun he found!

He bought _____ and _____ with his gold.

# St. Patrick's Patterns

Cut.

Complete each pattern.

Glue.

**Bonus Box:** Use the leftover pieces to create a pattern of your own on the back of your paper.

# IT'S A RAINBOW REVIEW!

Fun, appropriate reproducibles that review basic skills? They're out there. Just follow that rainbow!

### ADD A LITTLE COLOR

Addition facts take on new hues here. Duplicate page 34 for each child. Have him solve each problem and color the space according to the code. For added fun, provide colorful candies such as Skittles® to use as manipulatives and to munch on when finished.

### OVER THE RAINBOW

Your youngsters will be searching for similarities instead of gold with this game. Arrange all but one of your students' chairs in a circle. Designate one child to stand in the middle; then have the other children sit in the chairs. To play the game, the child in the middle says, "Over the rainbow I see people wearing [blue]." At that point, every child wearing blue—along with the child in the middle—has to find a new place to sit. The child left standing continues the game by saying the sentence and inserting a different color word. Continue until each child has had a turn to look over the rainbow!

### WHAT'S THE WORD?

The word is *color* in this activity. Duplicate page 35 and the pictures on page 36 for each child. Instruct the child to color the rainbow, then color each of the pictures according to its labeled color. Direct her to cut out the pictures and glue them to the corresponding beam in the rainbow. Color my world!

Name_____

## Add A Little Color

Write the sum.

Color by the code.

| | |
|---|---|
| 4—red | 7—blue |
| 5—orange | 8—green |
| 6—purple | 9—yellow |

$2 + 2 =$ _____

$3 + 1 =$ _____

$5 + 0 =$ _____

$2 + 3 =$ _____

$5 + 4 =$ _____

$2 + 7 =$ _____

$2 + 6 =$ _____

$3 + 2 =$ _____

$7 + 2 =$ _____

$3 + 5 =$ _____

$4 + 1 =$ _____

$4 + 5 =$ _____

$0 + 8 =$ _____

$7 + 0 =$ _____

$3 + 6 =$ _____

$6 + 2 =$ _____

$1 + 6 =$ _____

$8 + 1 =$ _____

$1 + 7 =$ _____

$5 + 2 =$ _____

$3 + 3 =$ _____

$4 + 4 =$ _____

$3 + 4 =$ _____

$4 + 2 =$ _____

Name: _____

## Color My World

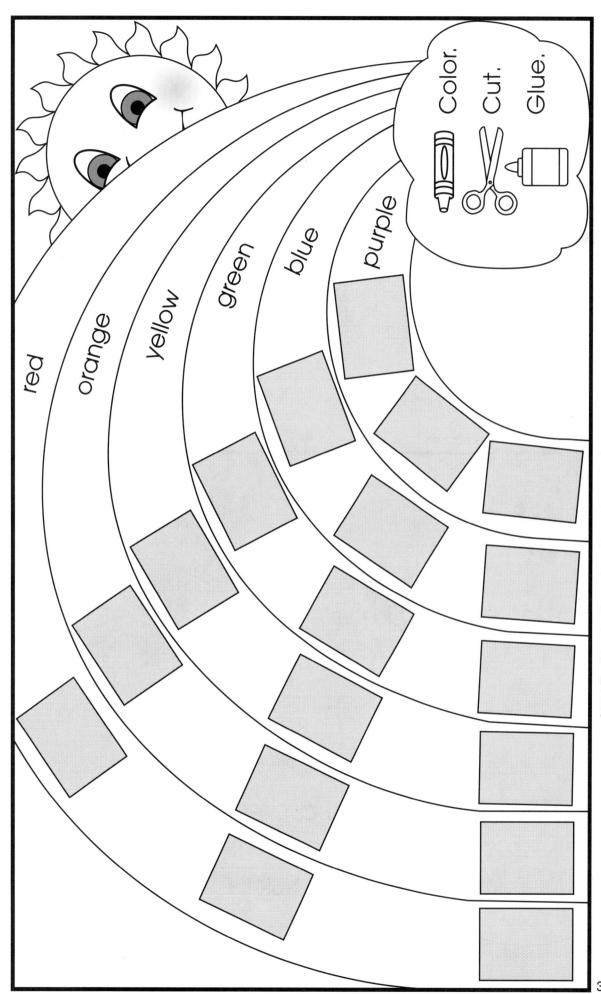

35

# Rainbow Pictures
Use with "Color My World" on page 35.

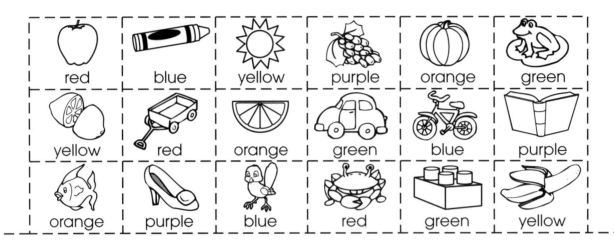

| | | | | | |
|---|---|---|---|---|---|
| red | blue | yellow | purple | orange | green |
| yellow | red | orange | green | blue | purple |
| orange | purple | blue | red | green | yellow |

# Award

Way To Go!

_____

did a great
job reviewing
basic skills.

_____ date

_____ teacher

# NATIONAL PEANUT MONTH

Give your youngsters an opportunity to go nuts with these fun peanut activities.

## The Peanut's Past

Share this nutty knowledge with your students as they nibble on some roasted-in-shell goobers.

- Peanuts, also called groundnuts, are native to South America.

- The peanut plant came to North America with the slave trade.

- After the Civil War, southern farmers began to grow more peanuts as a replacement for cotton crops that had been damaged by the boll weevil.

- George Washington Carver's extensive peanut research revealed over 300 uses for this soil-enriching plant and helped establish the peanut industry.

- Although America's most important peanut product is peanut butter, very little peanut butter is consumed in other countries.

- The majority of the worldwide peanut crop is used to make oil.

## I Like Peanuts!

Eat them here, eat them there, we eat peanuts everywhere! As a group, brainstorm a list of places that serve peanuts; then help each child construct this peanutty project.

Duplicate pages 38 and 39 onto white construction paper for each child. To make the project, draw red stripes on the peanut bag flaps. Color the peanuts at the top of the bag and the oval-shaped title. Then write your name in the rectangle. Next, color the illustrations and character pieces on page 39. Cut out the flaps, the set of illustrations, and the character pieces. Staple the flaps to the illustrations as indicated. Read the text; then glue each peanut character to its correct illustration. Finish the project by gluing real peanut shells to the top of the bag. After the glue dries, read the story again and again!

Eating Peanuts:
airplane
park
baseball game
movies
circus
party
mall

## Nutty Numbers

Counting to 20 gets quite crunchy in this "nut-rageous" game! Place a bowl of unshelled peanuts and a die in front of your group. Explain that the goal is to get exactly 20 peanuts out of the bowl. Have a volunteer roll the die and take the corresponding number of peanuts out of the bowl. Instruct the group to count the peanuts aloud. Have another volunteer roll the die and add the corresponding number of peanuts to the first amount. Direct the class to count the combined total. Continue this procedure until you reach 20. If the number of peanuts goes over 20, have the next student roll the die and *subtract* the corresponding number of peanuts from the group. As children get the hang of it, ask some problem-solving questions along the way, such as "How many more do we need to have 20?", "Is 18 more or fewer than 20?", and "Do we need to add or subtract?" Once 20 is reached, start over and play until each child has had a chance to participate. Store the game in the math center for students to revisit; then follow up the activity with the reproducible on page 40.

**Story Cover**
Use with "I Like Peanuts!" on page 37.

I like
peanuts...

by

_____

**Finished Sample**

Staple the left peanut bag flap here.

Staple the right peanut bag flap here.

...at the ball game.

...at the fair.

...at the circus.

...everywhere!

Name _____

# Nutty Numbers

Count.
Write the numeral.

**Bonus Box:** Draw 18 peanuts on the back of your paper.

# It's Time For The CIRCUS!

Telling time takes the center ring in these circus-themed activities.
So come one, come all, it's time to have a ball!

## Clown Clocks

Your youngsters will enjoy clowning around with time on these crafty clocks. To make one, duplicate the clock face and hand patterns on page 42 onto white construction paper and the hat and bow tie patterns on pages 43 and 44 onto colored construction paper. Color the clown's smile and nose; then color the clock's hands different colors to differentiate them. Next cut out the clock face and glue it to the back of a nine-inch paper plate. Cut out the clock's hands and attach them with a brad to the center of the clock where indicated. Punch three holes in the rim of the plate on each side of the face. Loop a seven-inch length of macramé cord or rug yarn through each of the holes as shown; then unravel the cord pieces to resemble a clown wig. Cut out the hat and bow tie. If desired, embellish them with sequins, glitter, pom-poms, stickers, etc. Then staple them to the paper plate rim. Tick-tock, what a clock!

## The Show Must Go On!

Continue to reinforce time-telling skills with the reproducibles on pages 45 and 46. The activities are self-explanatory and are perfect for individual practice.

## Rhyme Time

Invite youngsters to use their new clown clocks to show each of the times named in the following rhyme. Then duplicate the parent note on page 44. Send the clown clock and the parent note home to encourage more "time-ly" practice.

It's circus time, it's time for fun,
Just come along and see.
I'll show you how to tell the time,
As you spend the day with me.

It's 7:00—wake up, sleepyhead!
Chase the yawns away.
Brush your teeth and wash your face.
It's time to start the day.

It's 10:00—we're hard at work
Practicing for the show.
Juggling, tumbling, cycling, too,
Busy clowns on the go!

It's 12:00—get ready to eat.
It's time to have some lunch.
Peanut-butter sandwiches,
And cookies that go crunch.

It's 2:00—shh! Settle down,
Get comfy on your bed.
Take a nap while you can.
A busy night is ahead.

It's 5:00—oh my! Oh my!
It's time to get dressed.
Clothes, makeup, and wig just right.
Looking a clown's very best!

It's 8:00—it's show time!
The spotlight is on me.
Just listen to all of those hearty laughs.
I'm as happy as can be!

HA! HA! HA! HA! HA! HA!

# Clock Patterns
Use with "Clown Clocks" and "Rhyme Time" on page 41.

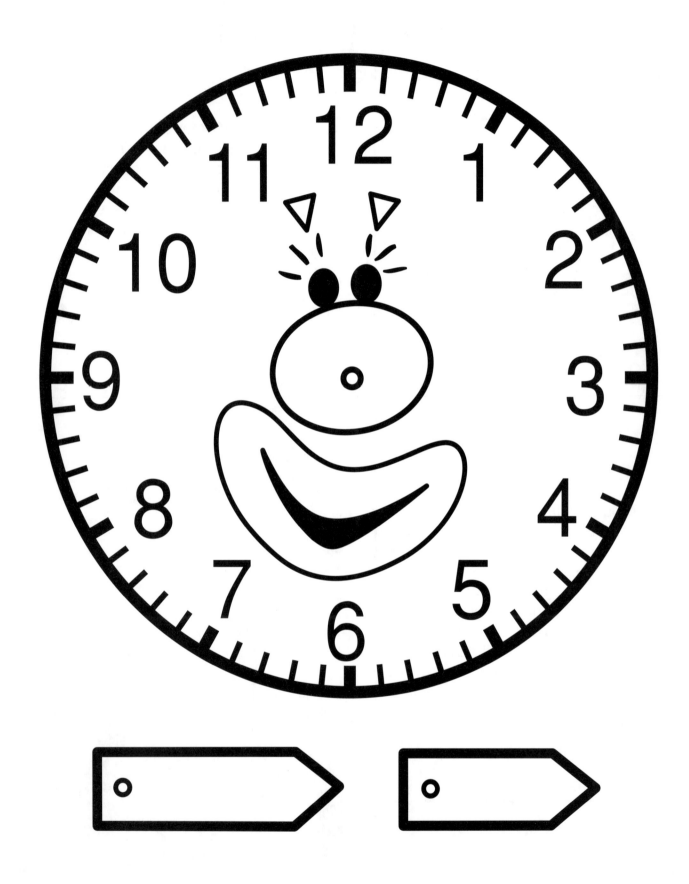

# Bow Tie Pattern
Use with "Clown Clocks" and "Rhyme Time" on page 41.

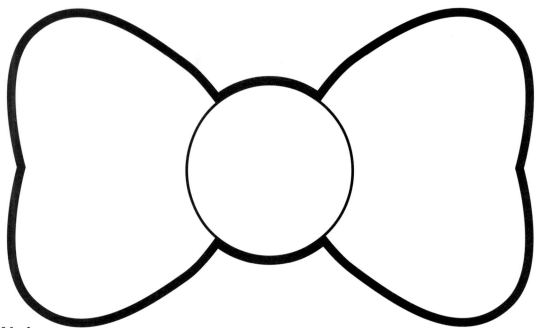

## Parent Note
Use with "Rhyme Time" on page 41.

Dear Parents,
   We've been clowning around with time! Please reinforce our time-telling efforts at home. Read the following rhyme as your youngster uses this clown clock to form the time for each verse. My, how time flies when you're having fun—and learning, too!

It's circus time, it's time for fun,
Just come along and see.
I'll show you how to tell the time,
As you spend the day with me.

It's 7:00—wake up, sleepyhead!
Chase the yawns away.
Brush your teeth and wash your face.
It's time to start the day.

It's 10:00—we're hard at work
Practicing for the show.
Juggling, tumbling, cycling, too,
Busy clowns on the go!

It's 12:00—get ready to eat.
It's time to have some lunch.
Peanut-butter sandwiches,
And cookies that go crunch.

It's 2:00—shh! Settle down,
Get comfy on your bed.
Take a nap while you can.
A busy night is ahead.

It's 5:00—oh my! Oh my!
It's time to get dressed.
Clothes, makeup, and wig just right.
Looking a clown's very best!

It's 8:00—it's show time!
The spotlight is on me.
Just listen to all of those hearty laughs.
I'm as happy as can be!

©1998 The Education Center, Inc.

©1998 The Education Center, Inc. • *March Monthly Reproducibles* • *Kindergarten* • TEC943

## Tower Of Time

Draw the clocks' hands to show the correct times.
Color the picture.

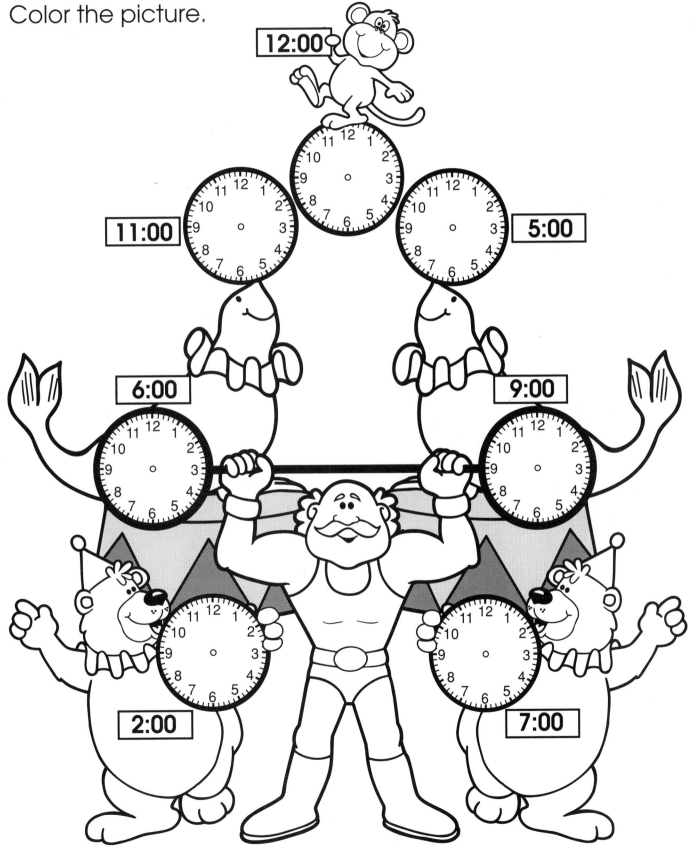

Name _____

# "Time-ly" Tigers

Cut.
Glue.
Color.

©1998 The Education Center, Inc. • *March Monthly Reproducibles* • Kindergarten • TEC943

46

| 11:30 | 4:30 | 1:30 | 8:30 |
| 7:30 | 9:30 | 12:30 | 3:30 |

# YOUTH ART MONTH

Use the following activities to explore art with your youngsters in recognition of March as Youth Art Month.

## The "Art" Of Storytelling

Share these fun stories about children and their artistic talents. Your little ones will enjoy hearing about and relating to young artists just like themselves.

***Pearl Paints***
Written by Abigail Thomas
Published by Henry Holt And Company, Inc.

***Regina's Big Mistake***
Written by Marissa Moss
Published by Houghton Mifflin Company

***Almost Famous Daisy!***
Written by Richard Kidd
Published by Simon & Schuster Books For Young Readers

***The Art Lesson***
Written by Tomie dePaola
Published by G. P. Putnam's Sons

***Incredible Ned***
Written by Bill Maynard
Published by G. P. Putnam's Sons

## The Eyes Have It!

Help your youngsters understand that art is a way of seeing or, in other words, that three people can look at the same picture and see something totally different. Show several abstract works of art and discuss them with your students. Does everyone have the same ideas? Of course not! Give each child a white construction-paper copy of page 48. Encourage him to use crayons (or other mixed media) to turn the printed shapes into a fascinating masterpiece and display the finished works of art on a bulletin board titled "Art Is A Way Of Seeing."

47

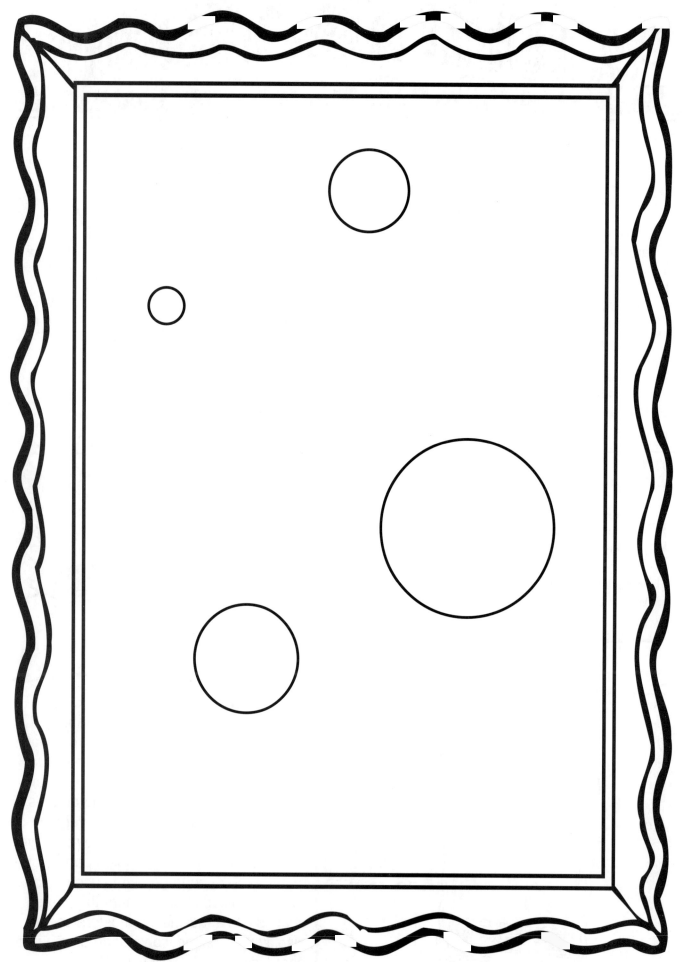

# MUSIC IN OUR SCHOOLS MONTH

Sound the trumpets! March has been designated as Music In Our Schools Month. Sing music education's praises with these harmonious activities.

## Strike Up The Band

Whether at a football game or a parade, marching bands are always a hit. Invite your youngsters to strike up their own bands with this booklet idea. For each child, duplicate pages 50–54 onto white construction paper. (If desired, you may want to duplicate the back cover on page 54 onto tagboard for sturdiness.) Each child will also need scissors, crayons, glue, two brads, access to a black washable ink pad, and access to a stapler. Help create and assemble the booklets using the following directions.

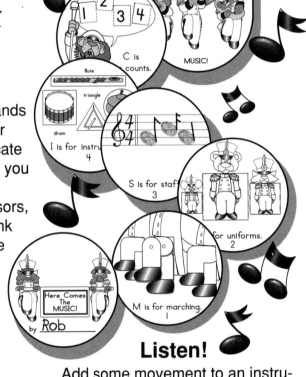

1. Color and cut out the front cover. Write your name in the space provided.
2. Color and cut out page 1 and the leg pieces. Fasten the leg pieces together at the Xs with one of the brads. Then use the other brad to attach the leg to the page where indicated.
3. Color and cut out page 2 and the uniform pieces. Glue each uniform to its corresponding wearer.
4. Cut out page 3. Make several black fingerprints on the staff. Then draw lines with a black crayon next to the prints to resemble music notes.
5. Color and cut out page 4 and the musical instruments. Glue the instruments in their correct spaces.
6. Color and cut out page 5. Cut out the numerals. Glue them in the correct order where indicated.
7. Color and cut out the back cover.
8. Stack the pages and covers sequentially and staple them together at the top.

When the booklets are completed, read the text aloud. Encourage your youngsters to take their booklets home to share with their families.

## Listen!

Add some movement to an instrumental selection and you'll have an awesome integrated activity that will receive demands for repeat performances. Choose a selection of music that has obvious changes in volume, tempo, or instruments. Pick two movements, such as twisting and bouncing or clapping and stomping. Explain to your youngsters that each time the music changes, they are to change movements. Then play the music and start moving…encore, encore!

49

**Front Cover**
Use with "Strike Up The Band" on page 49.

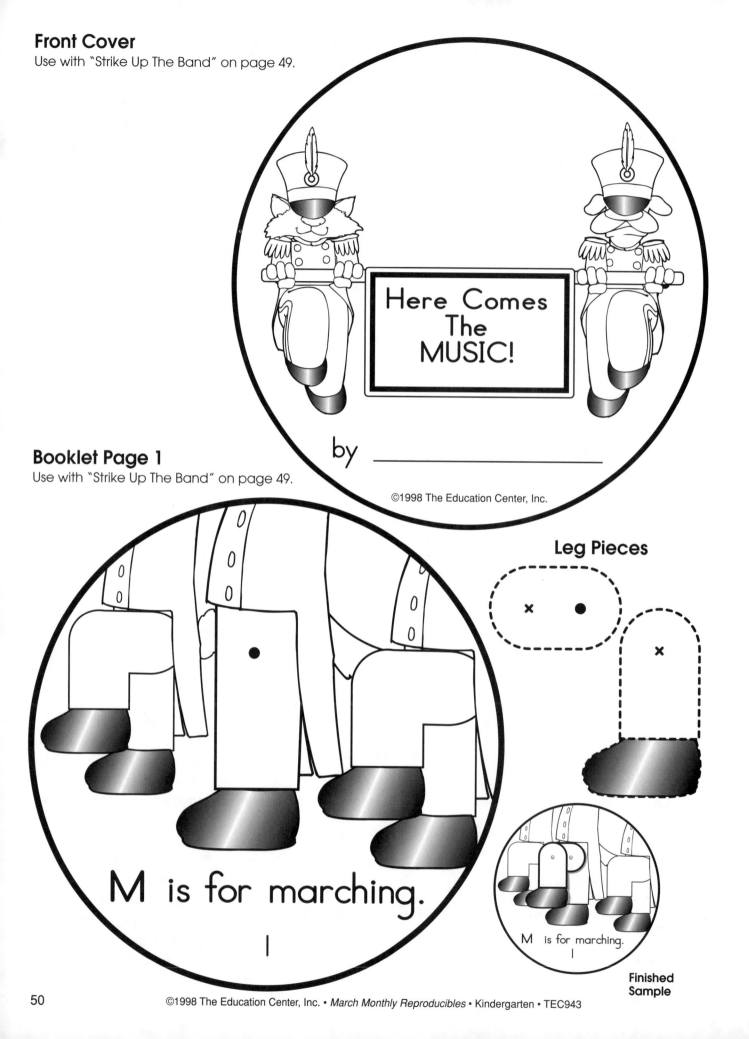

Here Comes
The
MUSIC!

by _____

**Booklet Page 1**
Use with "Strike Up The Band" on page 49.

**Leg Pieces**

M is for marching.

1

**Finished Sample**

U is for uniforms.

2

**Booklet Page 3**
Use with "Strike Up The Band" on
page 49.

S is for staff.

3

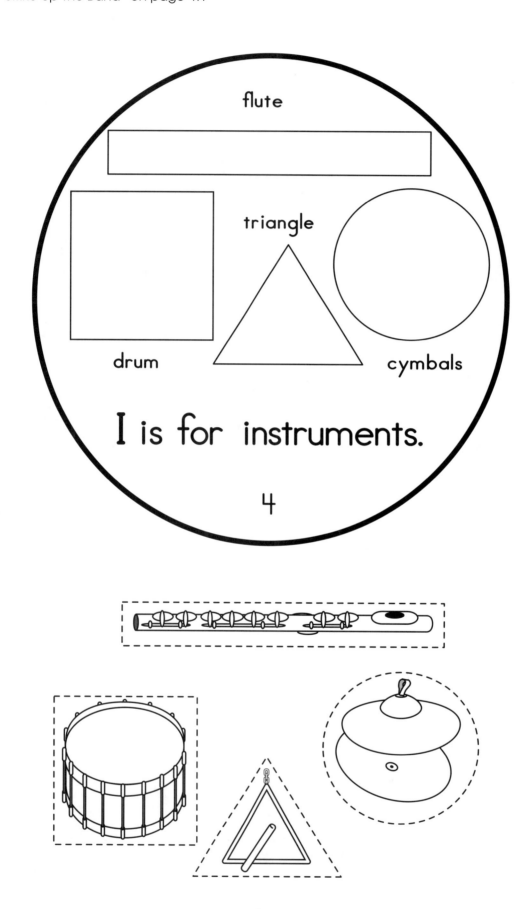

flute

triangle

drum

cymbals

I is for instruments.

4

C is
for counts.

5

1  2  3  4

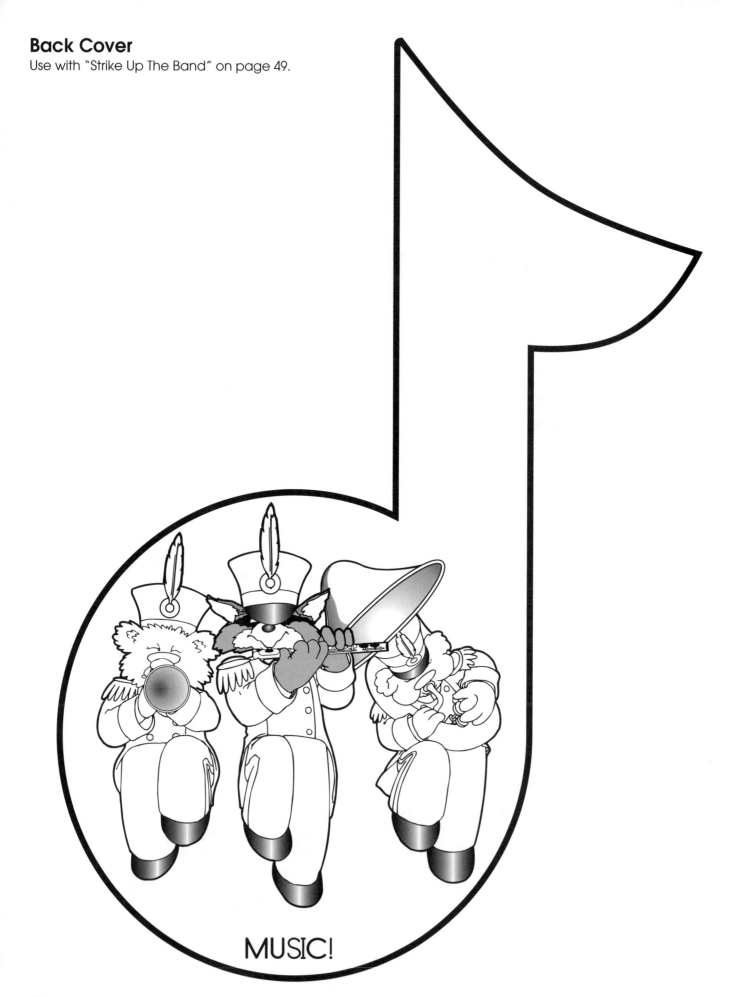

MUSIC!

# The March Wind Blows...

...and blows and blows! Use the following activities for some classroom fun on a windy day.

## Windy Windsocks

A windy day is a perfect day to make and use these nifty windsocks. To prepare, duplicate page 56 onto white construction paper for each child. Purchase a few rolls of colored crepe-paper streamers. Cut two 20" lengths of yarn for each child. Then make sure each child has access to scissors, crayons, a hole puncher, a stapler, and glue.

To make a windsock, color and cut out the two strips from page 56. Punch four holes in the tops of the strips where indicated. Staple the strips together to form a cylinder as shown. Then cut six streamers in assorted colors and lengths and glue them to the bottom of the inside of the cylinder. Thread each piece of yarn through a pair of opposing holes. Then gather all four ends and tie them into a knot for hanging.

## Whose Kite?

The answer is blowing in the wind as youngsters practice their addition to reveal whose kite is whose. Give each child a copy of page 58 and five 6" strands of yarn—each strand being a different color. Instruct the child to solve each problem, then glue a strand of yarn to connect the character with the corresponding kite. Trim the strands' excess lengths; then have the youngster color the pictures to complete the page.

## Hold On To Your Hat!

Don't let basic skills get blown away! Duplicate page 57 for each child. Have her cut out the hat pieces and glue each of them to its correct owner. Each animal should be wearing the hat that's labeled with the initial sound of its name—for example, the sheep would wear the hat labeled with **sh**.

# Windsock Pattern

Use with "Windy Windsocks" on page 55.

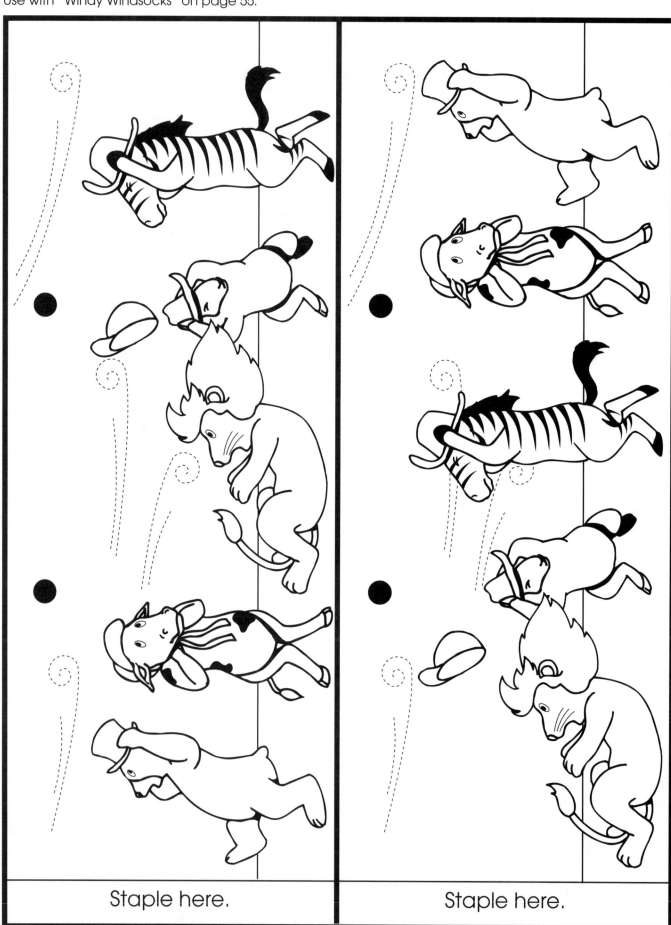

Staple here.                    Staple here.

## Hold On To Your Hat!

Name the animal.
Cut out the hat that is labeled with the animal's beginning sound.
Glue.

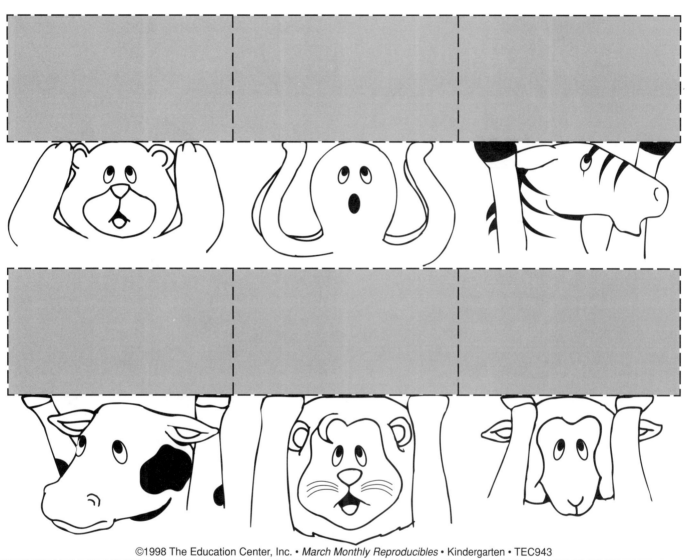

©1998 The Education Center, Inc. • *March Monthly Reproducibles* • Kindergarten • TEC943

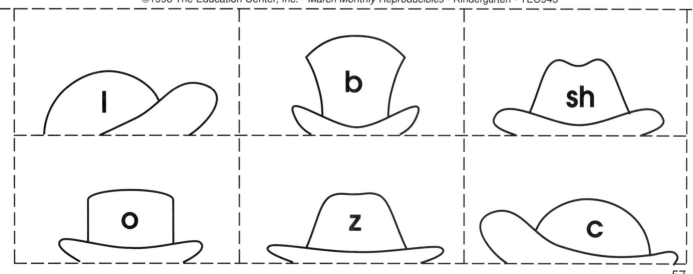

# Whose Kite?

Solve the problem.
Glue yarn to connect the problem to its correct sum.

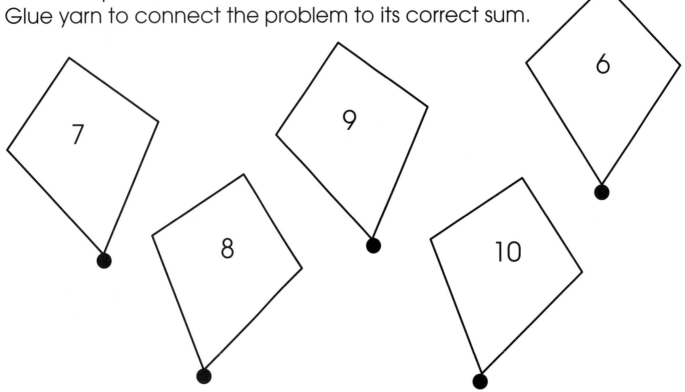

©1998 The Education Center, Inc. • *March Monthly Reproducibles* • Kindergarten • TEC943

# SPRING!

Ahh, the feel of the warm sun, the sound of chirping birds, the smell of fresh-cut grass—it must be spring! Use this refreshing collection of activities to make everyone say, "So long, winter—hello, spring!"

## A Spring Scene

Do your little ones have spring fever? This math activity is just what the doctor ordered. Duplicate the math mat and manipulatives on pages 60 and 61 onto white construction paper for each child. Invite him to color the pages, then cut out the mat and cut apart the manipulatives. (You may want to laminate both pages for durability before cutting.) Have him use his mat and manipulatives to do the following activities. If desired, make overhead transparencies of the sheets for your demonstrations or for a whole-group activity.

- Dramatize and solve story problems. For example, "Three bunnies hopped out of the log and met four frogs by the pond. How many animals are there in all?"
- Make patterns using two or three of the animal and flower sets.
- Practice positional words by following oral directions. For example, "Put two butterflies to the right of the big tree. Put five flowers at the bottom of the page."
- Work on ordinal numbers by positioning manipulatives in a specific verbalized order.

## Spring Things

Classification is the key here as your students sort through the seasons. Duplicate page 62 for each child. Have her cut out the pieces, then glue only the spring things to the corresponding places on the page. If time permits, encourage the child to draw her favorite spring thing on the back of her paper.

## A Nice Spring Day

Using the patterns on page 63, make flannelboard figures to illustrate the following poem fashioned after the traditional "This Little Piggy" rhyme. Once your little ones are familiar with the new verse, give each of them a copy of page 64 to complete and take home to share with their families. Yea, yea, yea, it's a nice spring day!

This little chick just hatched.
This little chick stays warm.
This little chick eats worms.
This little chick pecks for corn.
And this little chick peeps, "Yea, yea, yea, it's a nice spring day!"

Name_____

# Spring Things

Cut.

Glue.

Color.

# A Nice Spring Day

 Cut.

Read the rhyme.

Glue each illustration to its corresponding sentence.

This little chick just hatched.

This little chick stays warm.

This little chick eats worms.

This little chick pecks for corn.

And this little chick peeps,
"Yea, yea, yea, it's a nice spring day!"